Ellarese Harvey Present:

Be Unique

Adult Coloring Book
with
Self Encouraging Quotes

KPLA Publishing

Be Unique - Adult Coloring Book with Self-Encouraging Quotes
ISBN 13 – 978-1-943833-17-7
ISBN 10 - 1-943833-17-6
Copyright 2017 © by Ellarese L. Harvey

Published by:
KPLA Publishing – Kissed Publications
PO Box 9819
Hampton, VA 23670
www.kplapublishing.com

10 9 8 7 6 5 4 3 2 1

Give thanks
for unknown
blessings are
already on
their way.

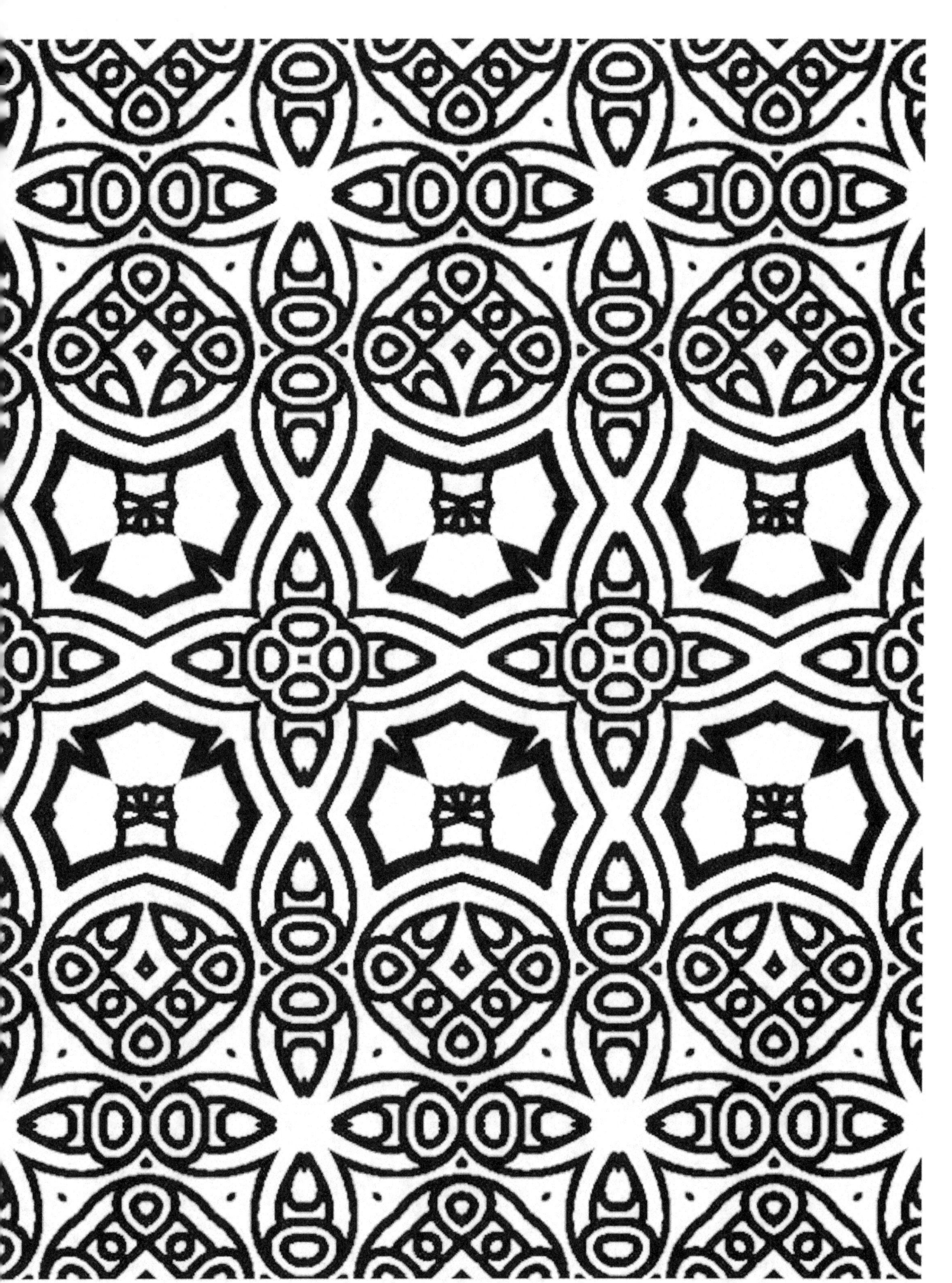

The positive thinker...

sees the invisible,

feels the intangible

and

achieves the impossible.

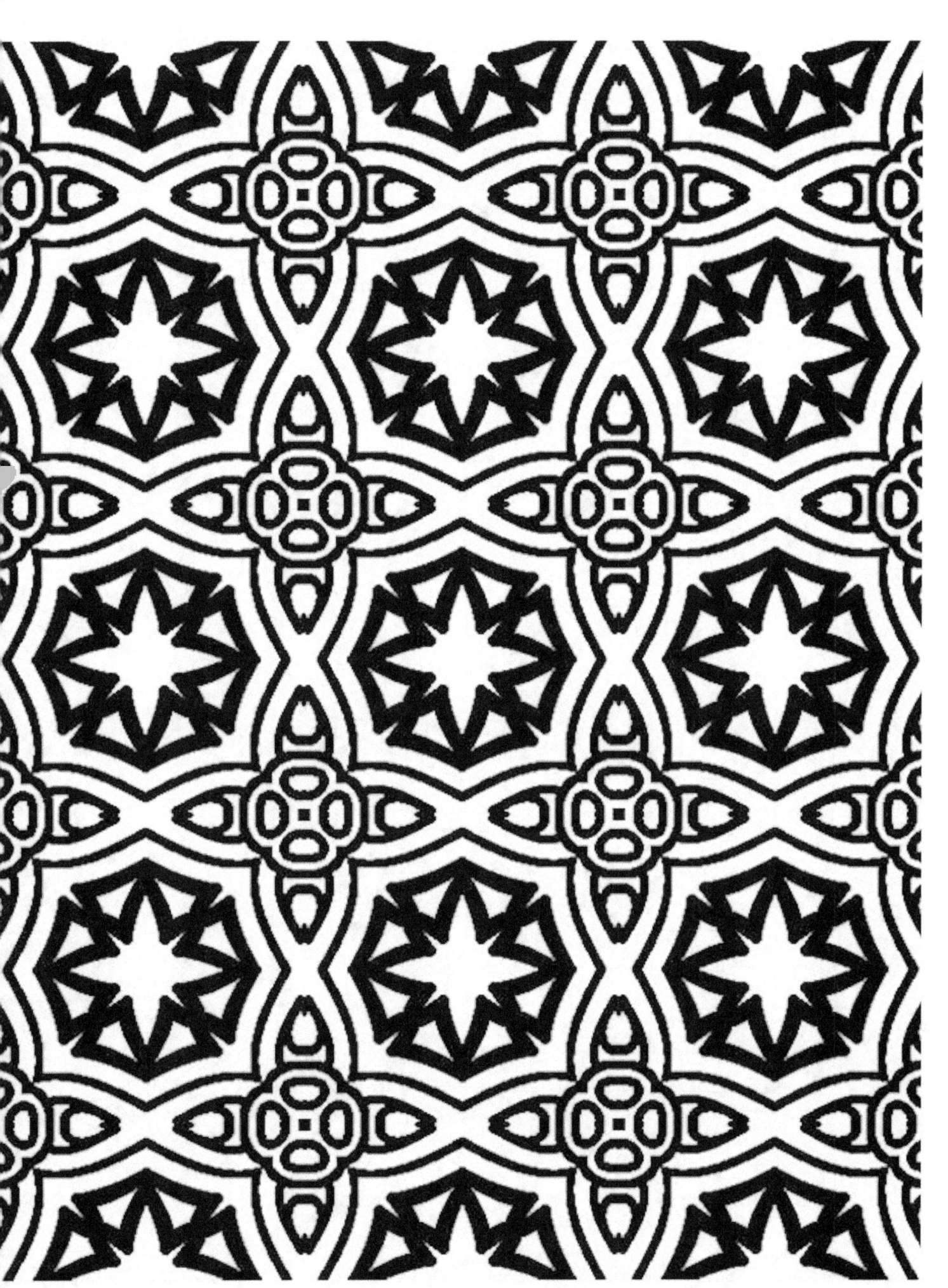

It's not selfish to love yourself, take care of yourself and to make your happiness a priority... It's necessary.

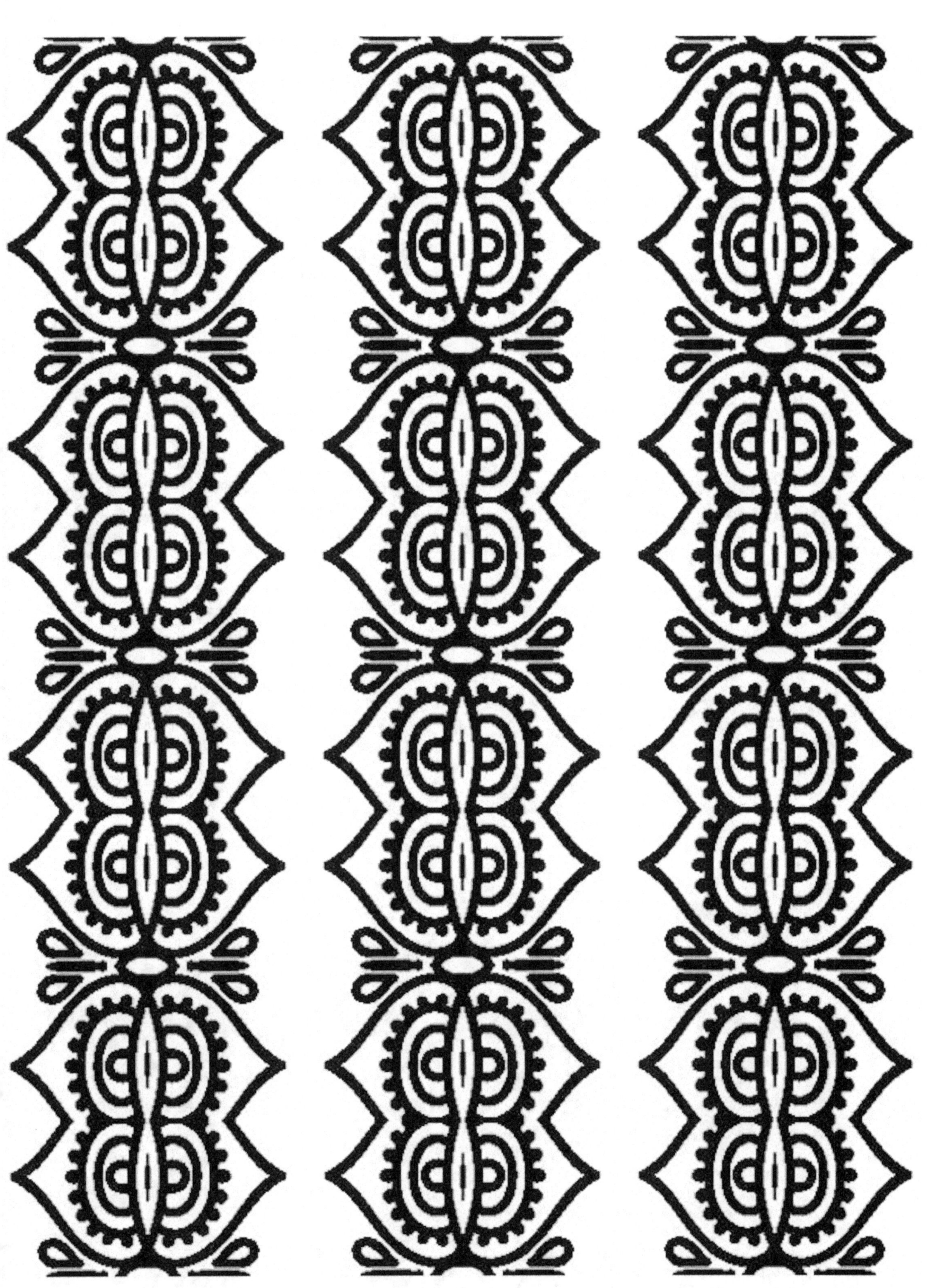

Love yourself, for if you don't how can you expect anyone else to love you

Collect moments, not things.

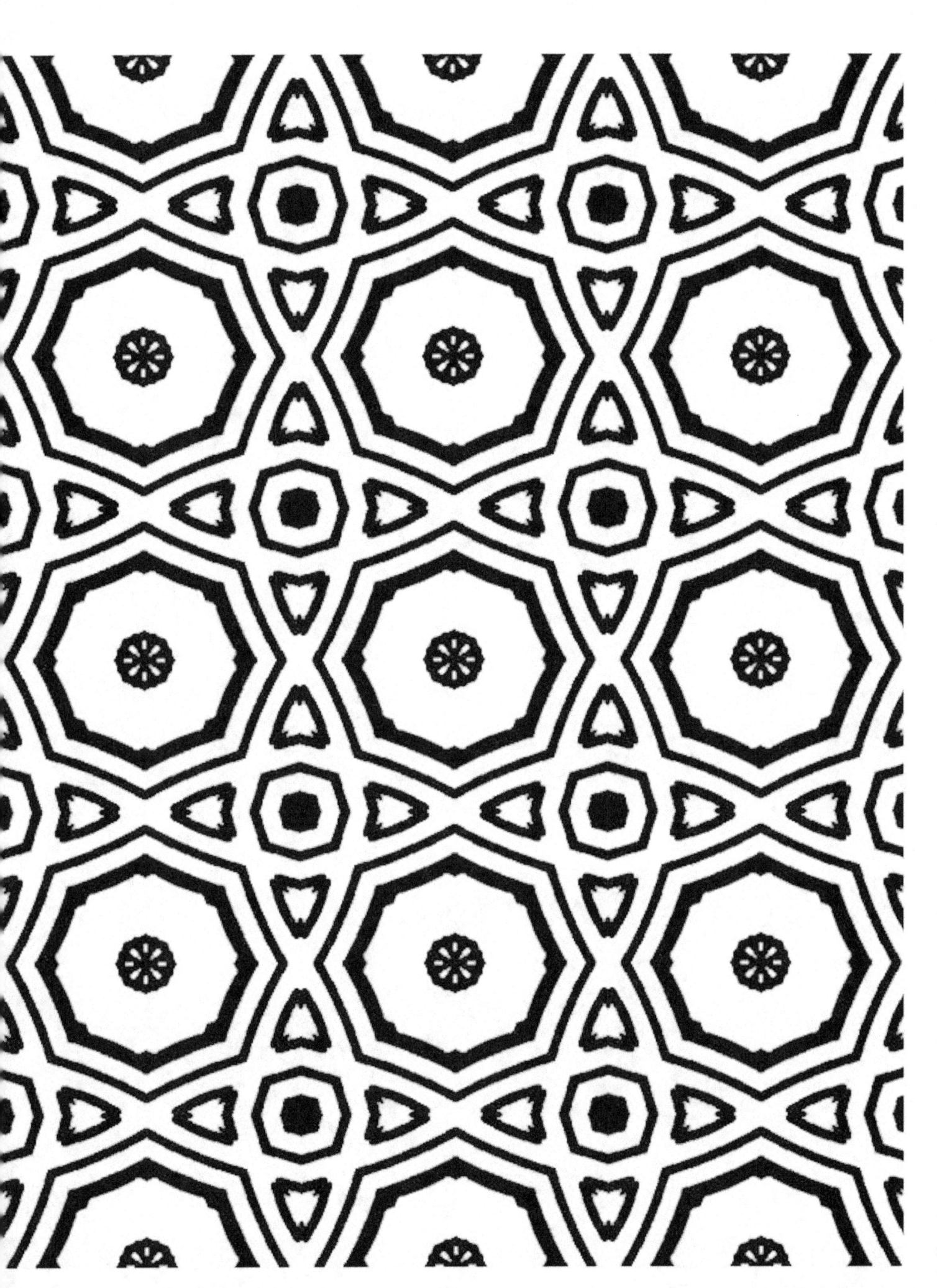

Always remember that your present situation is not your final destination. The best is yet to come.

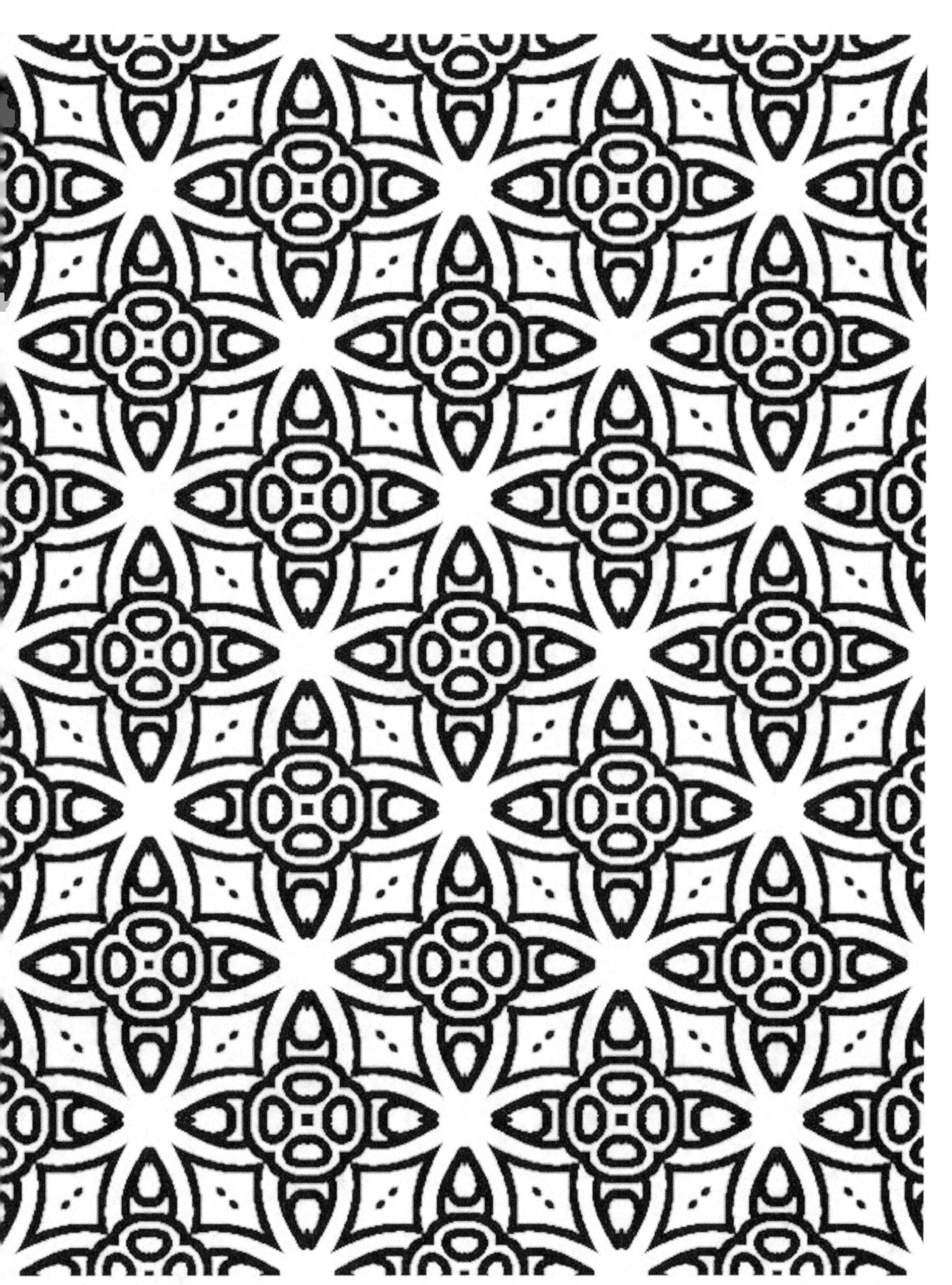

At my lowest... God is my Hope.

At my darkest... God is my Light.

At my weakest... God is my Strength.

At my saddest... God is my Comforter.

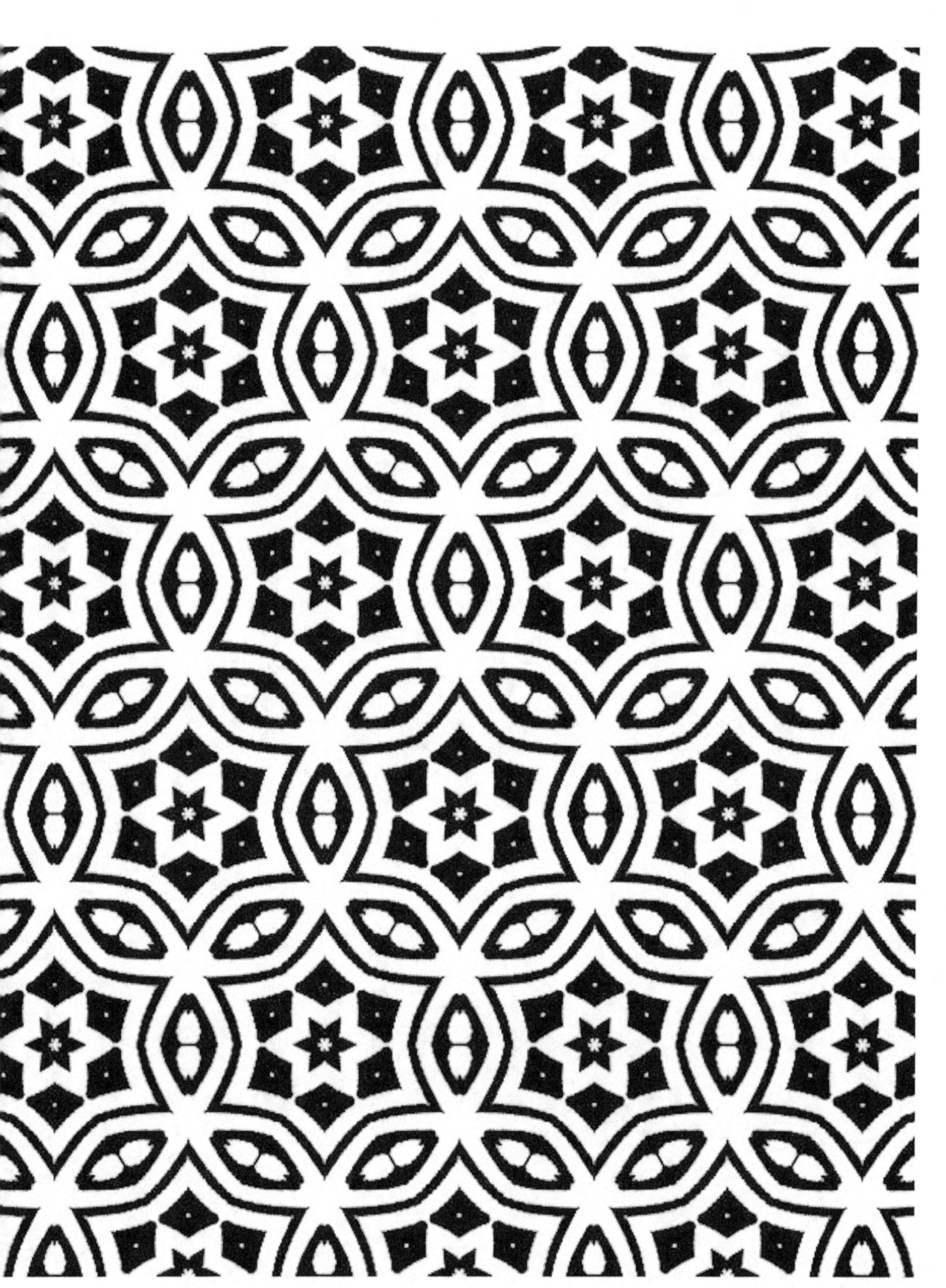

Be yourself, be natural. It is far easier than pretending to be someone else.

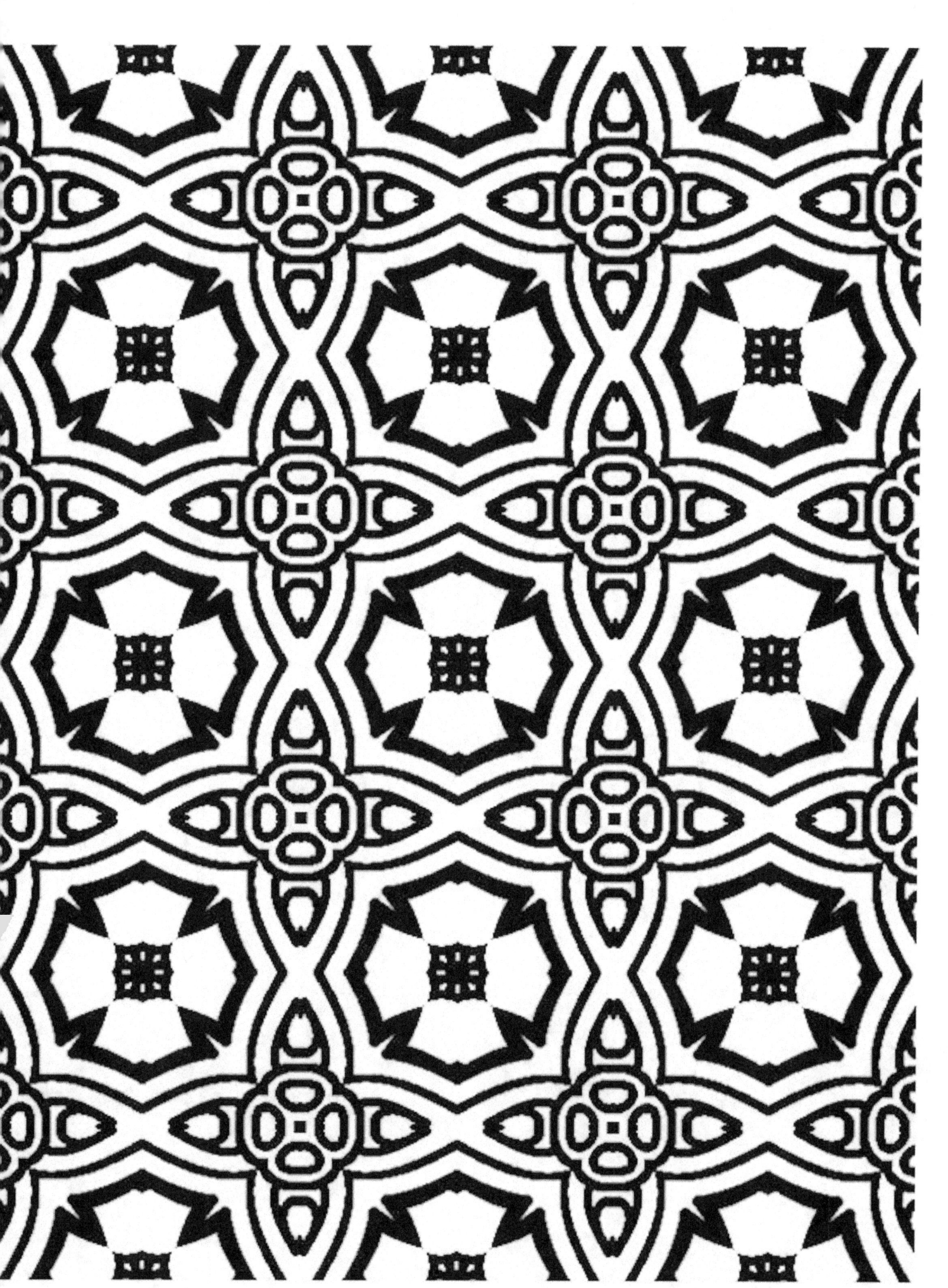

Be yourself, be natural. It is far easier than pretending to be someone else.

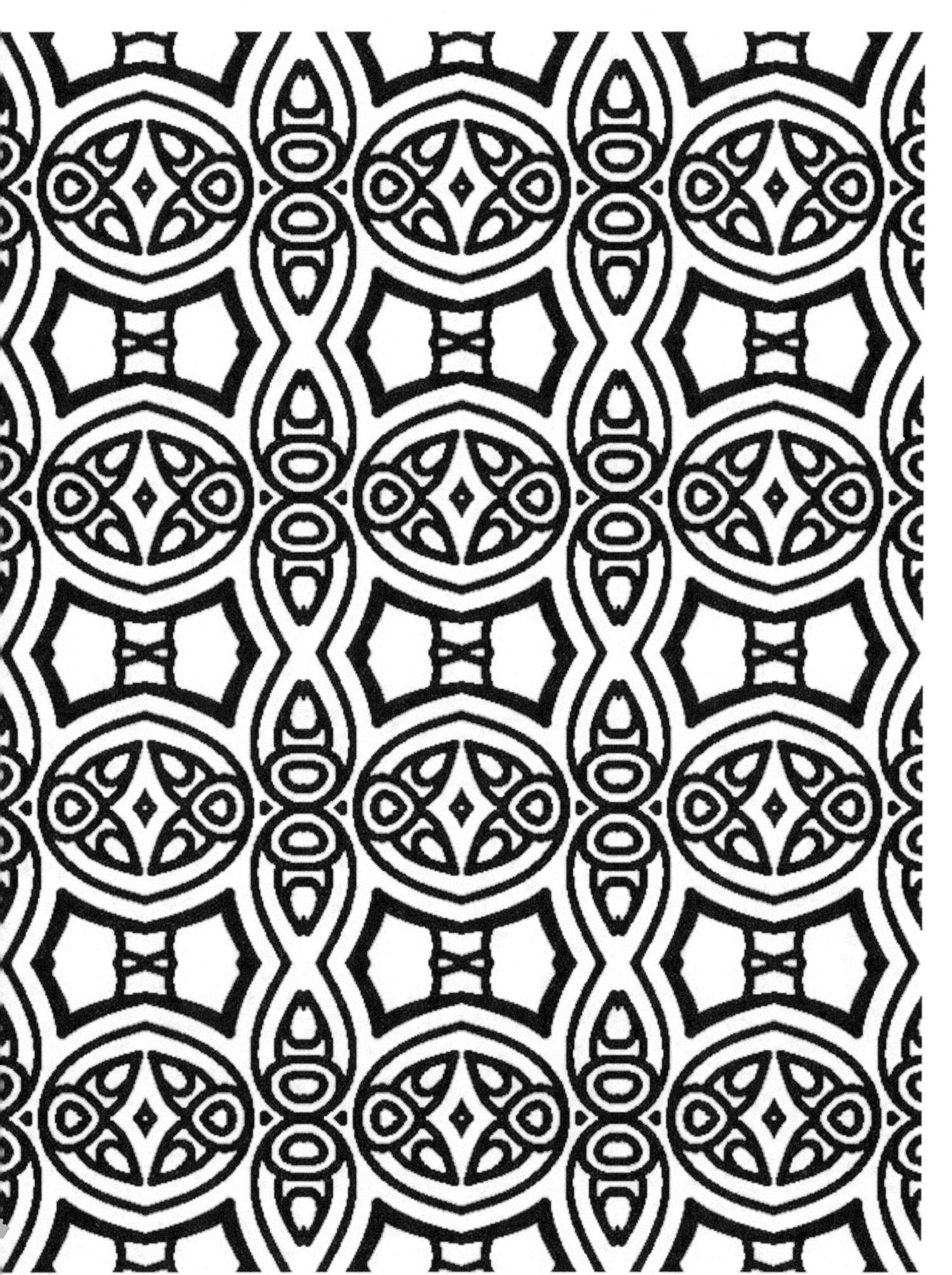

By being yourself, you put something wonderful in the world, that was not there before.

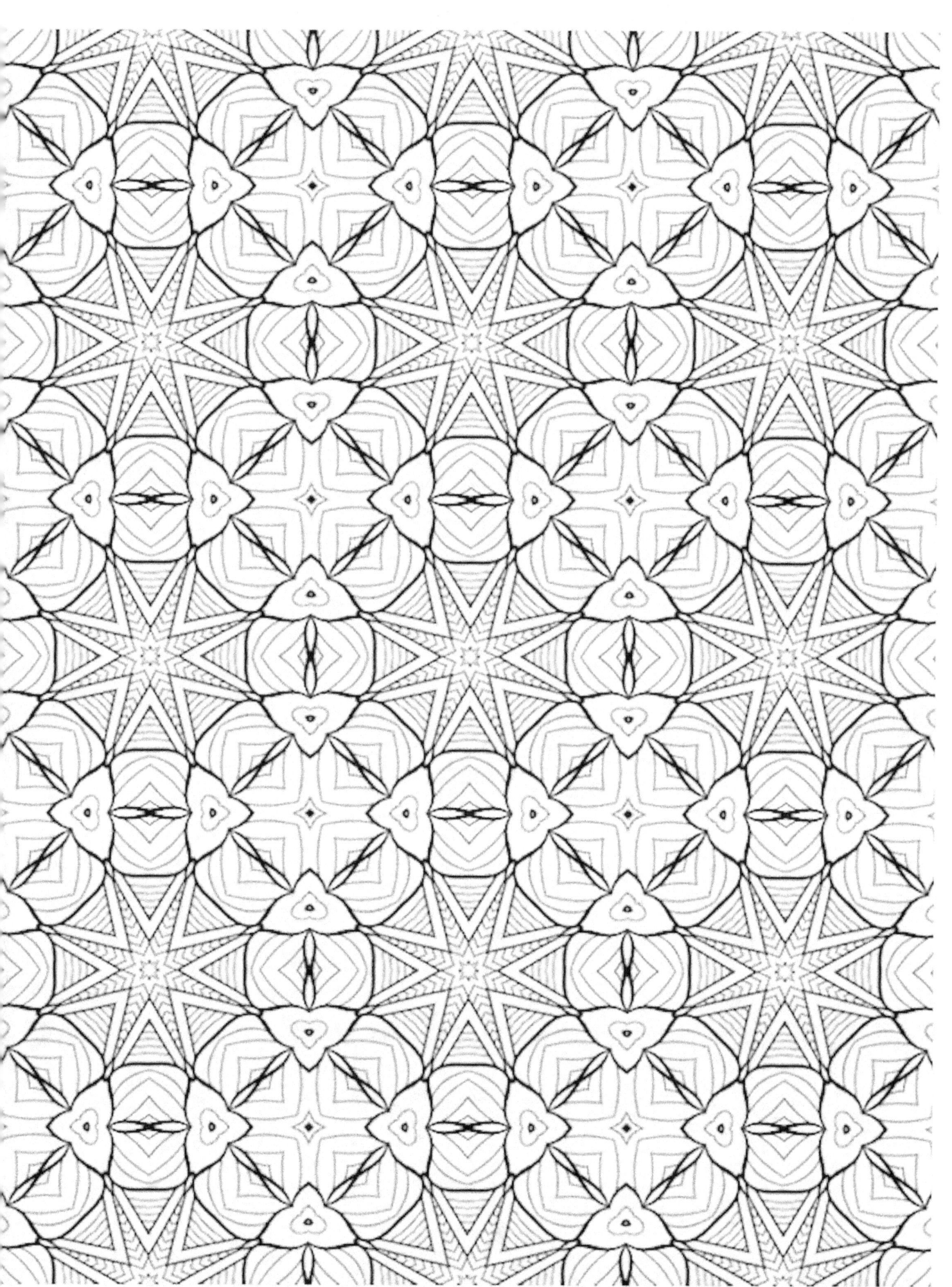

Don't change
so people will like you.
Be yourself
and the right people
will love you.

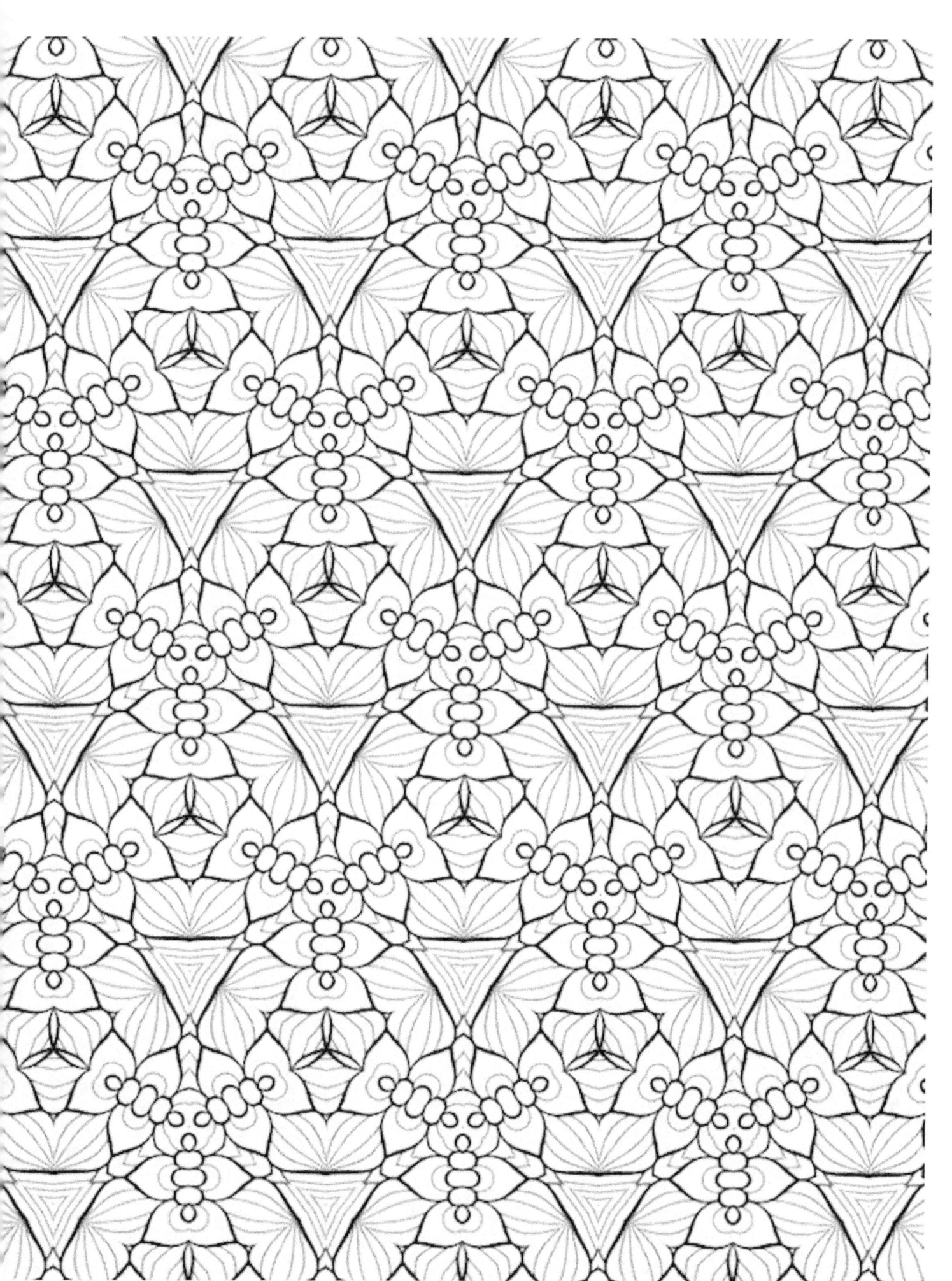

Don 't compare or

compete...

Be unique.

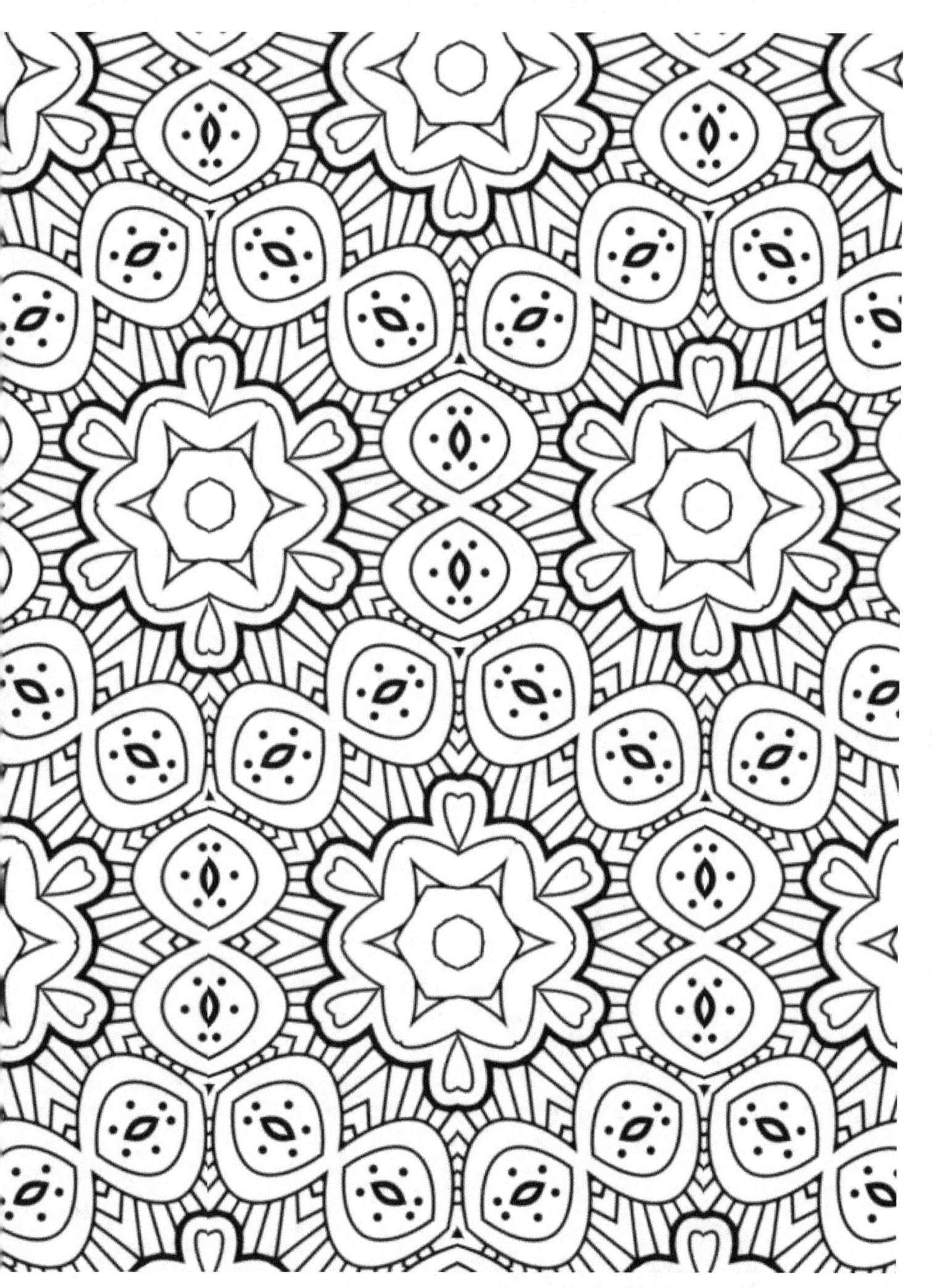

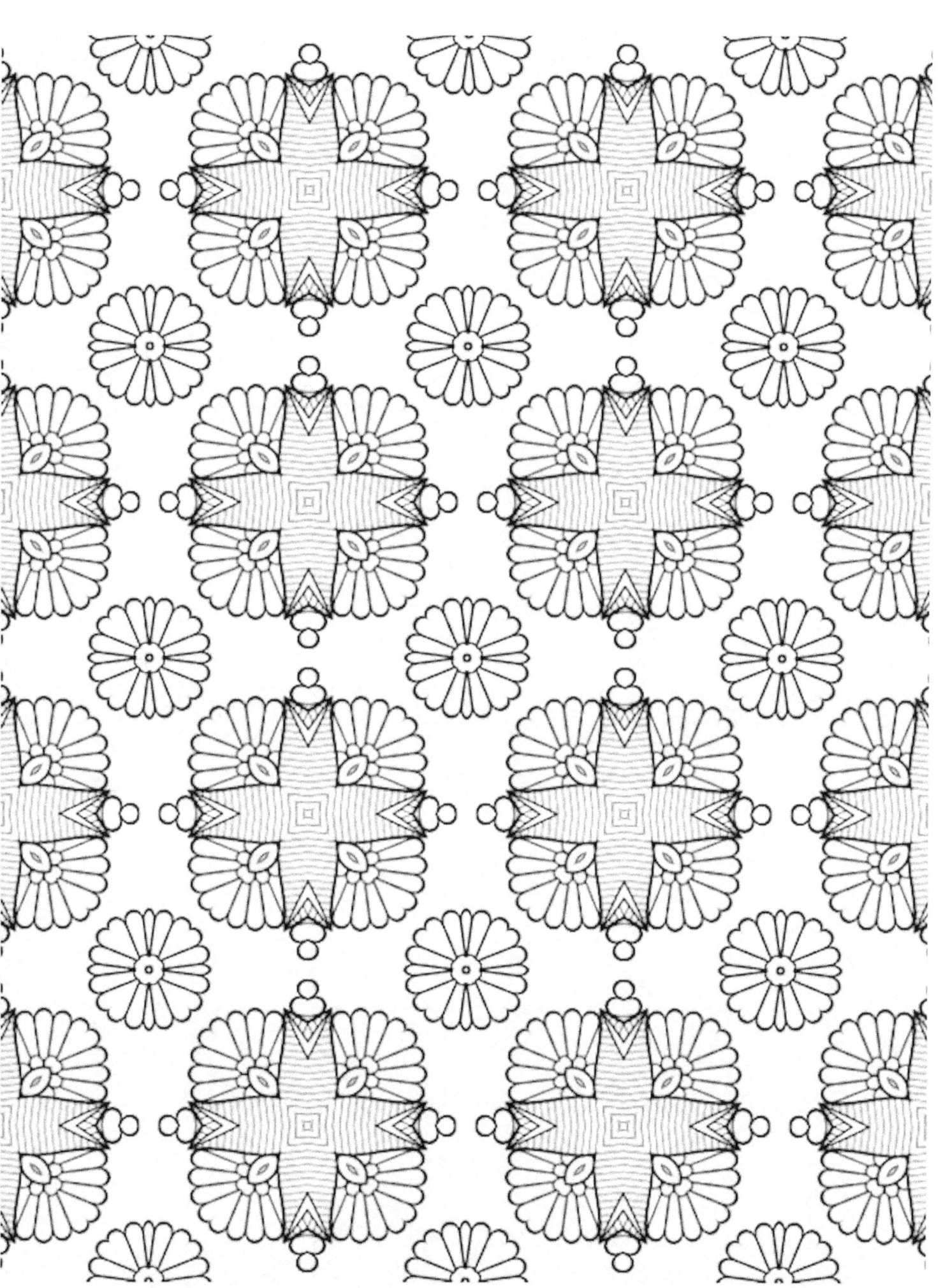

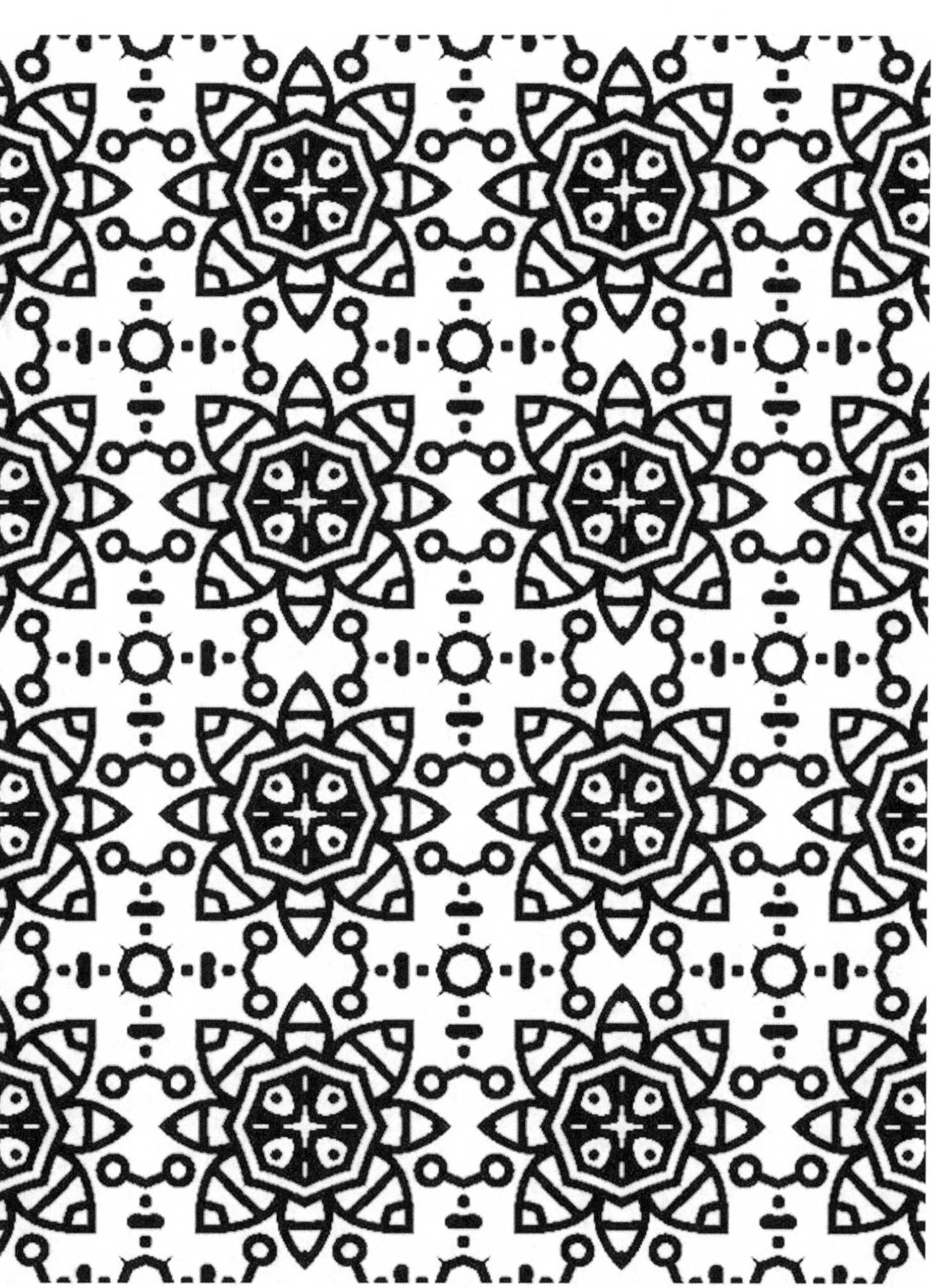

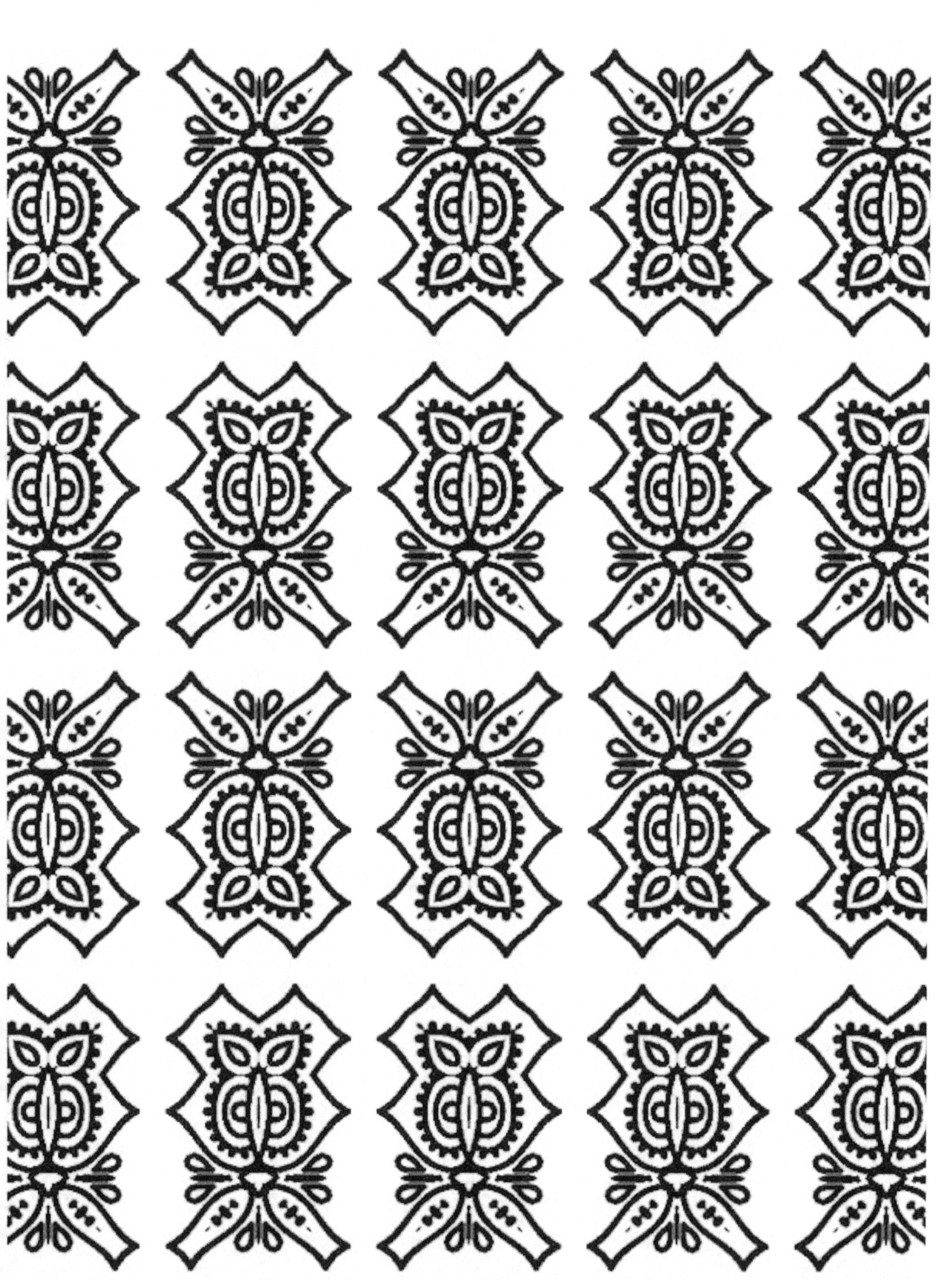

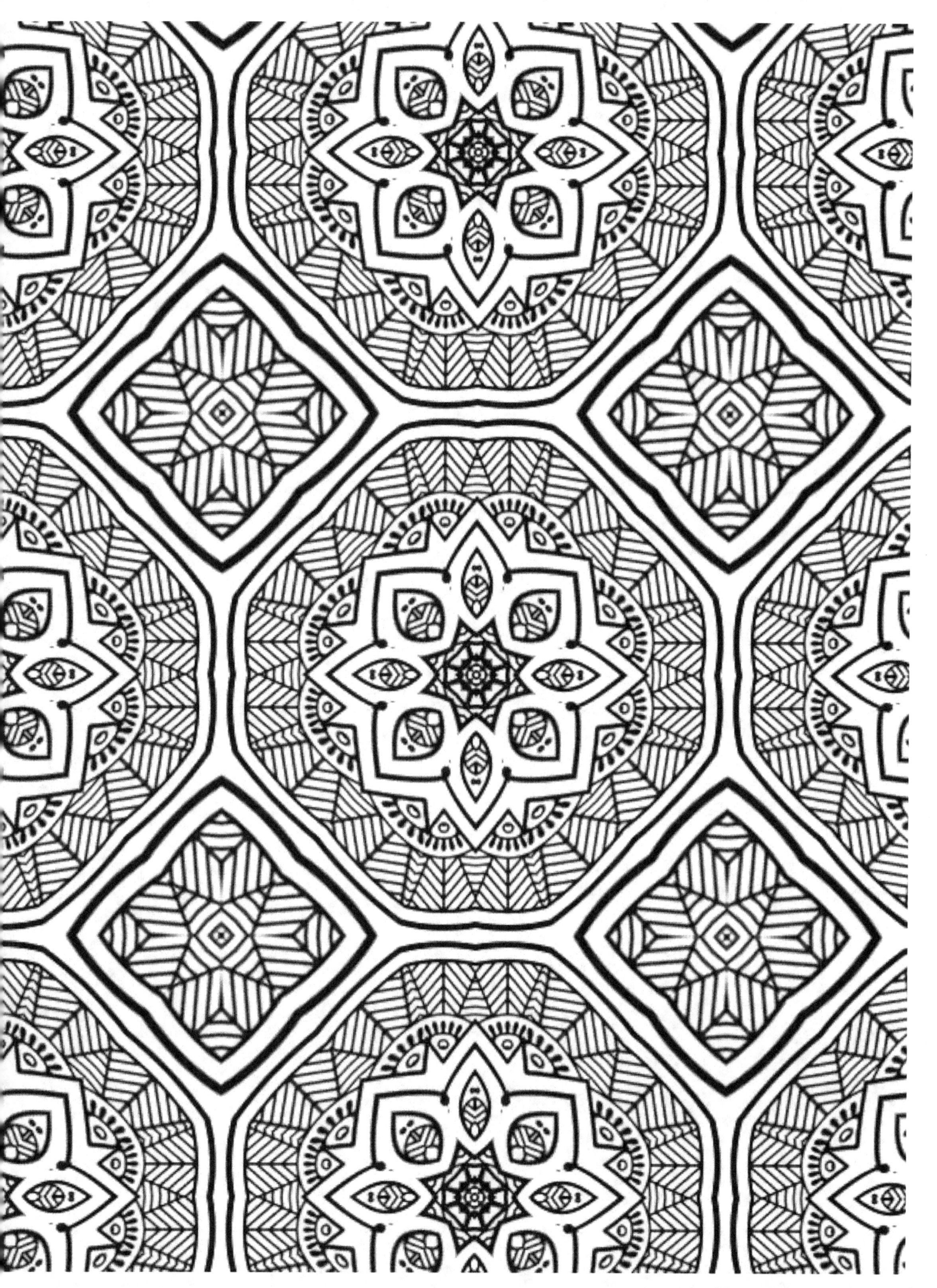

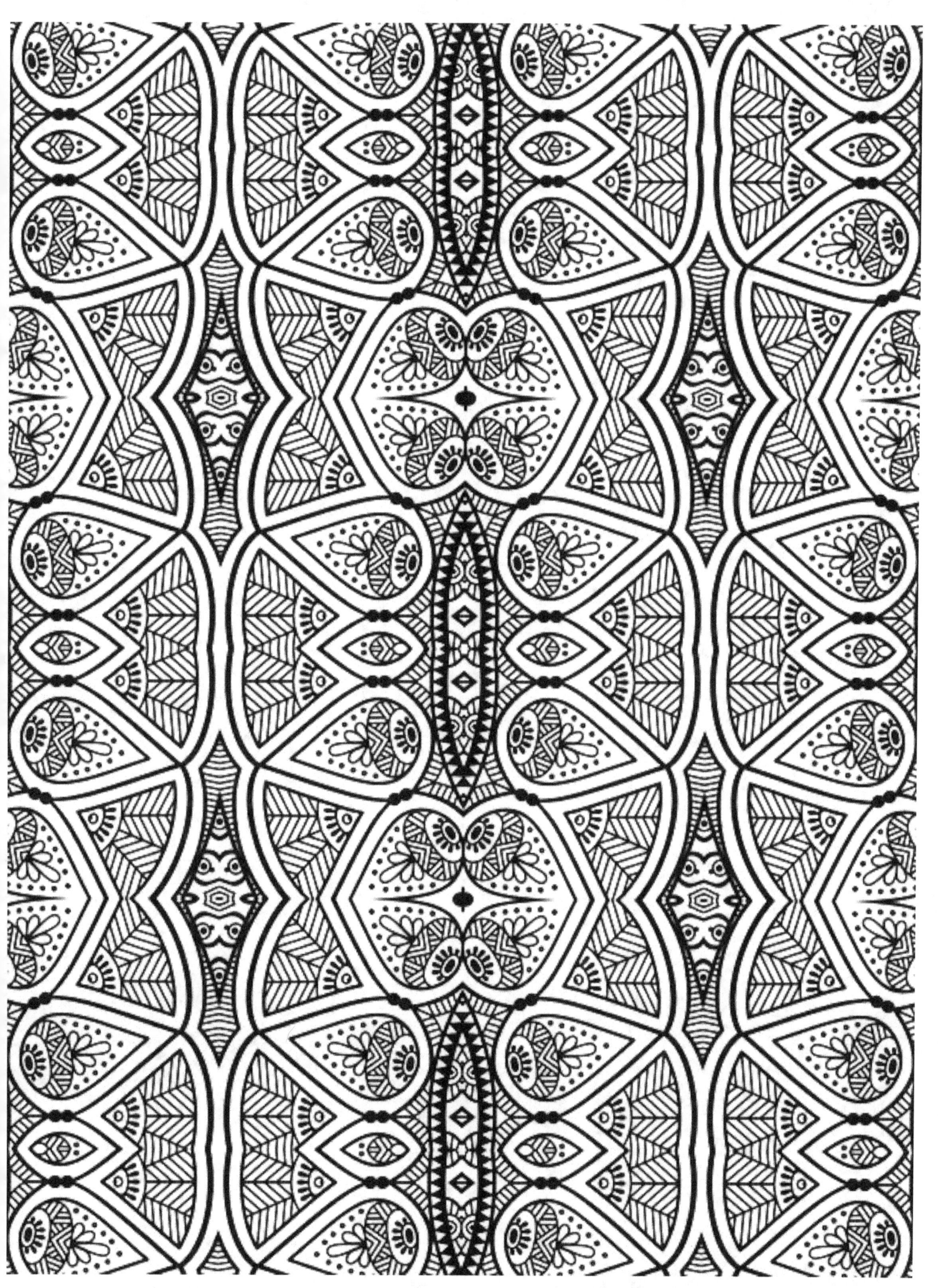

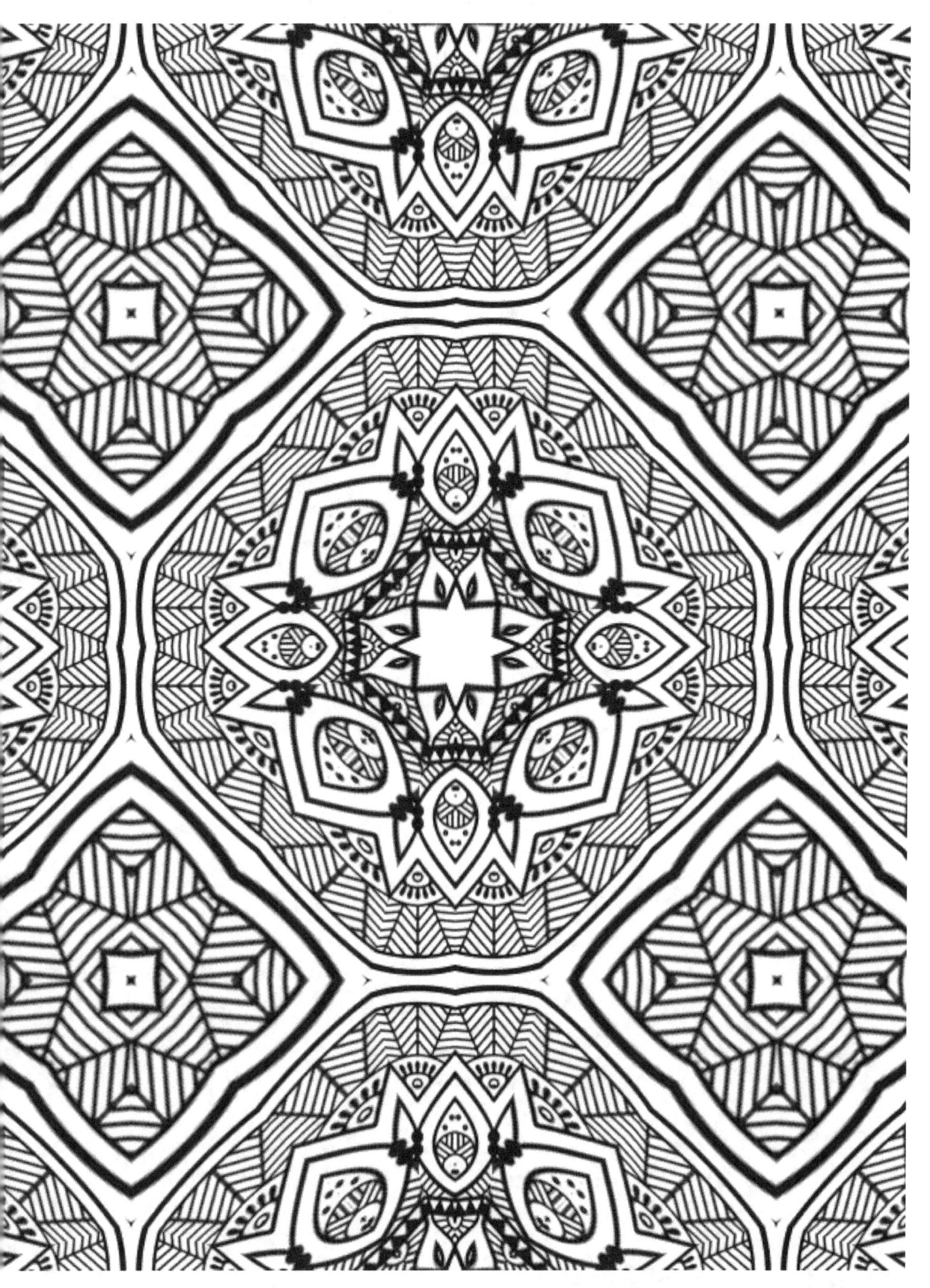

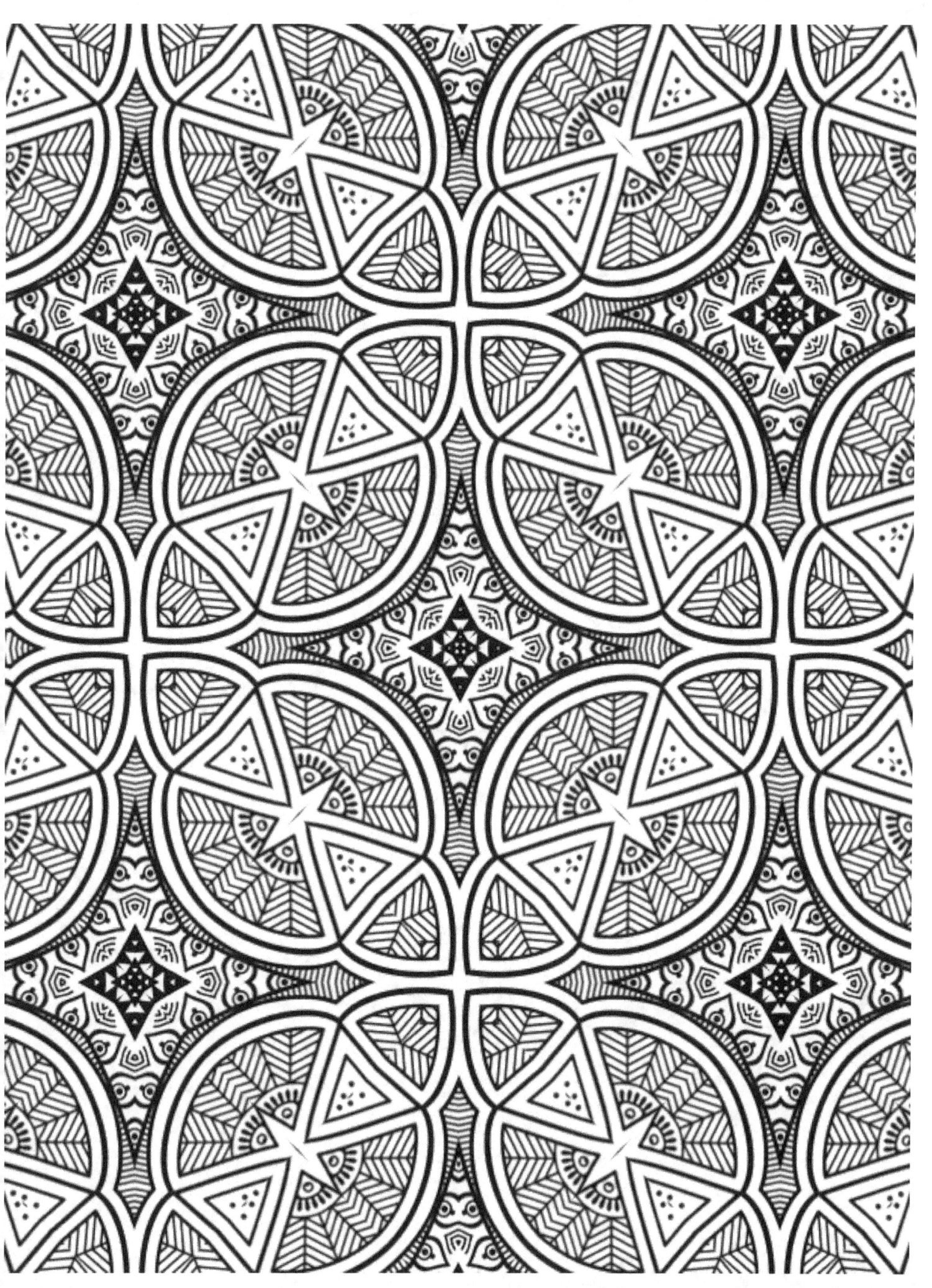

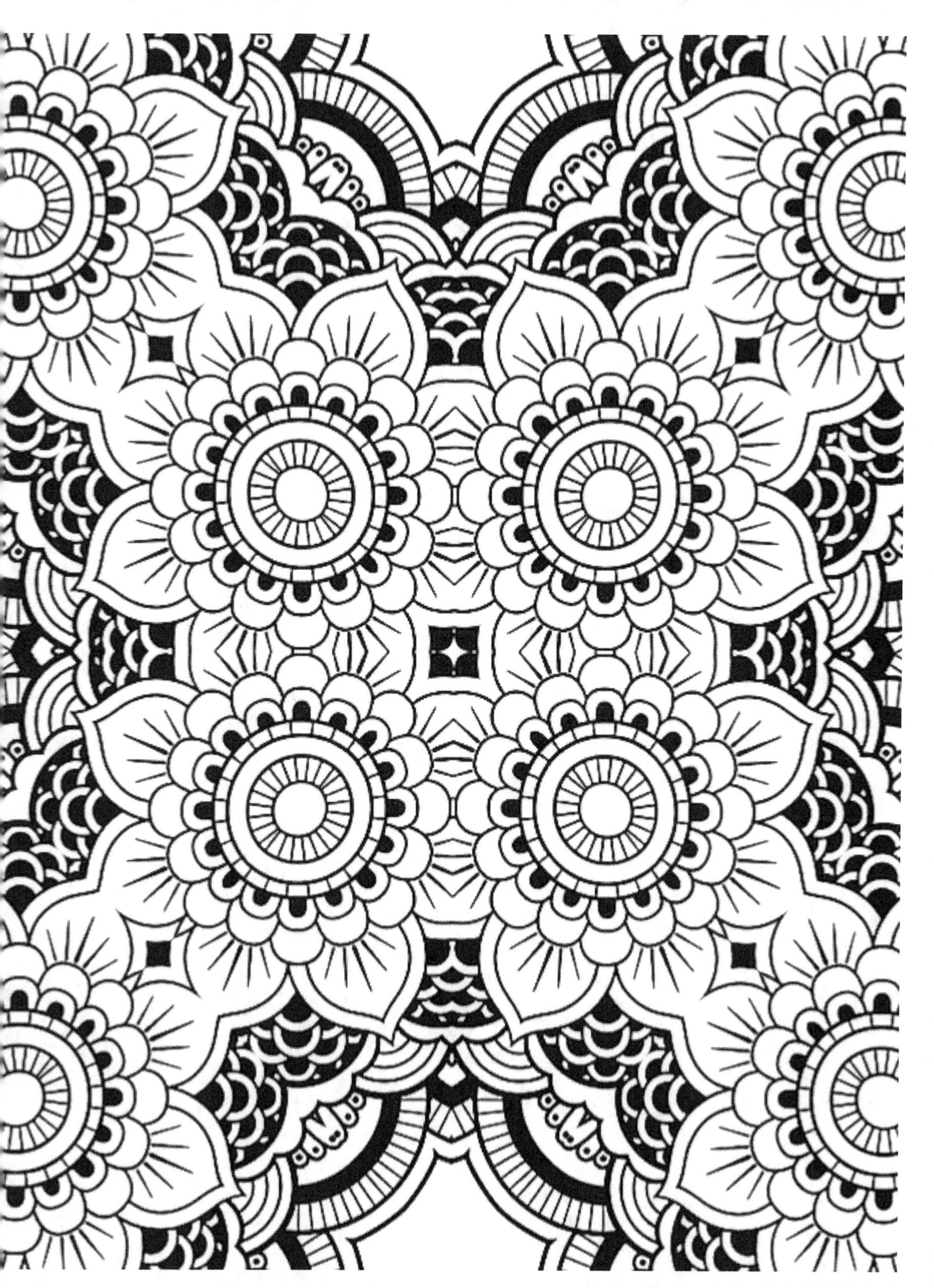

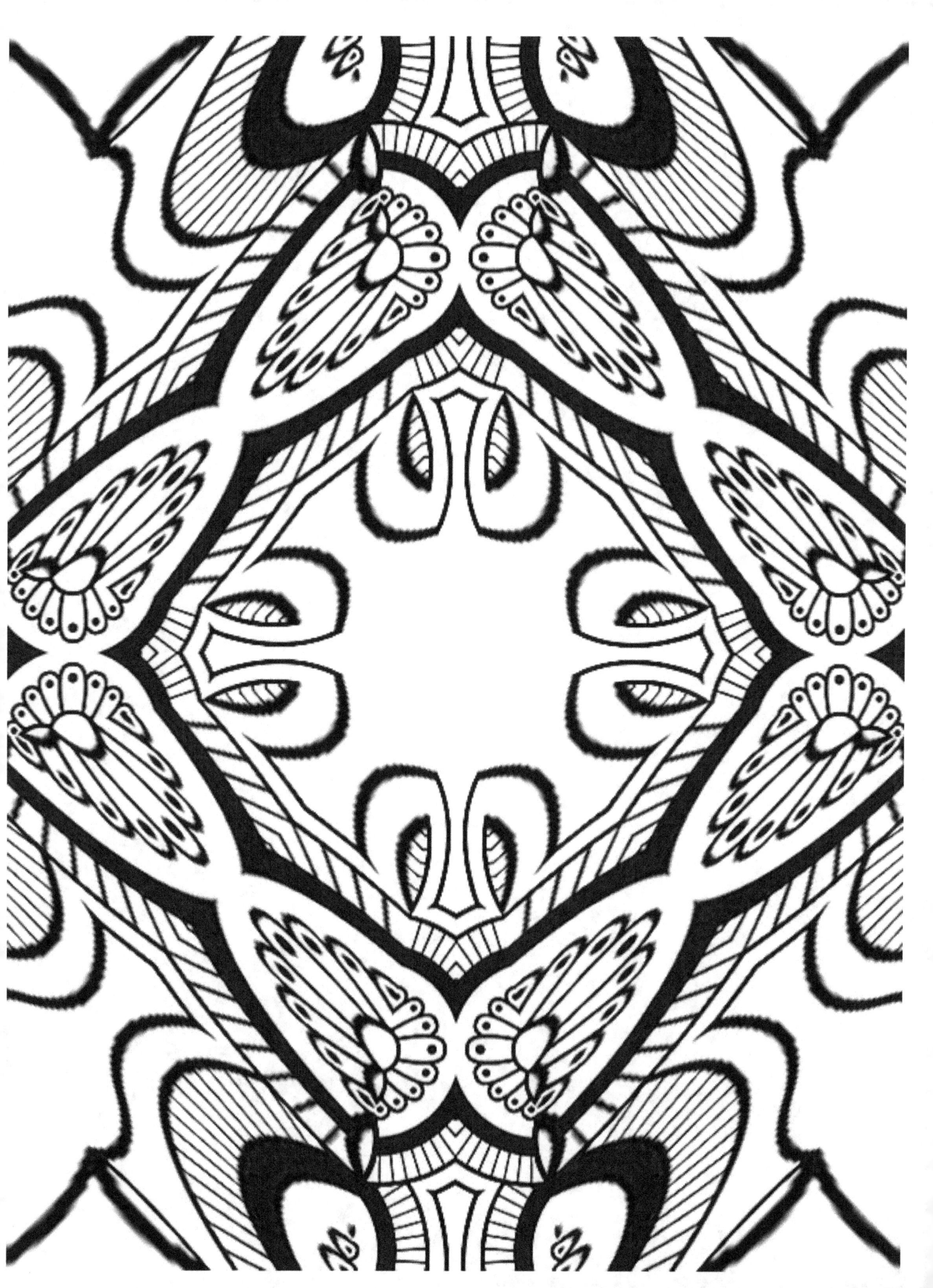

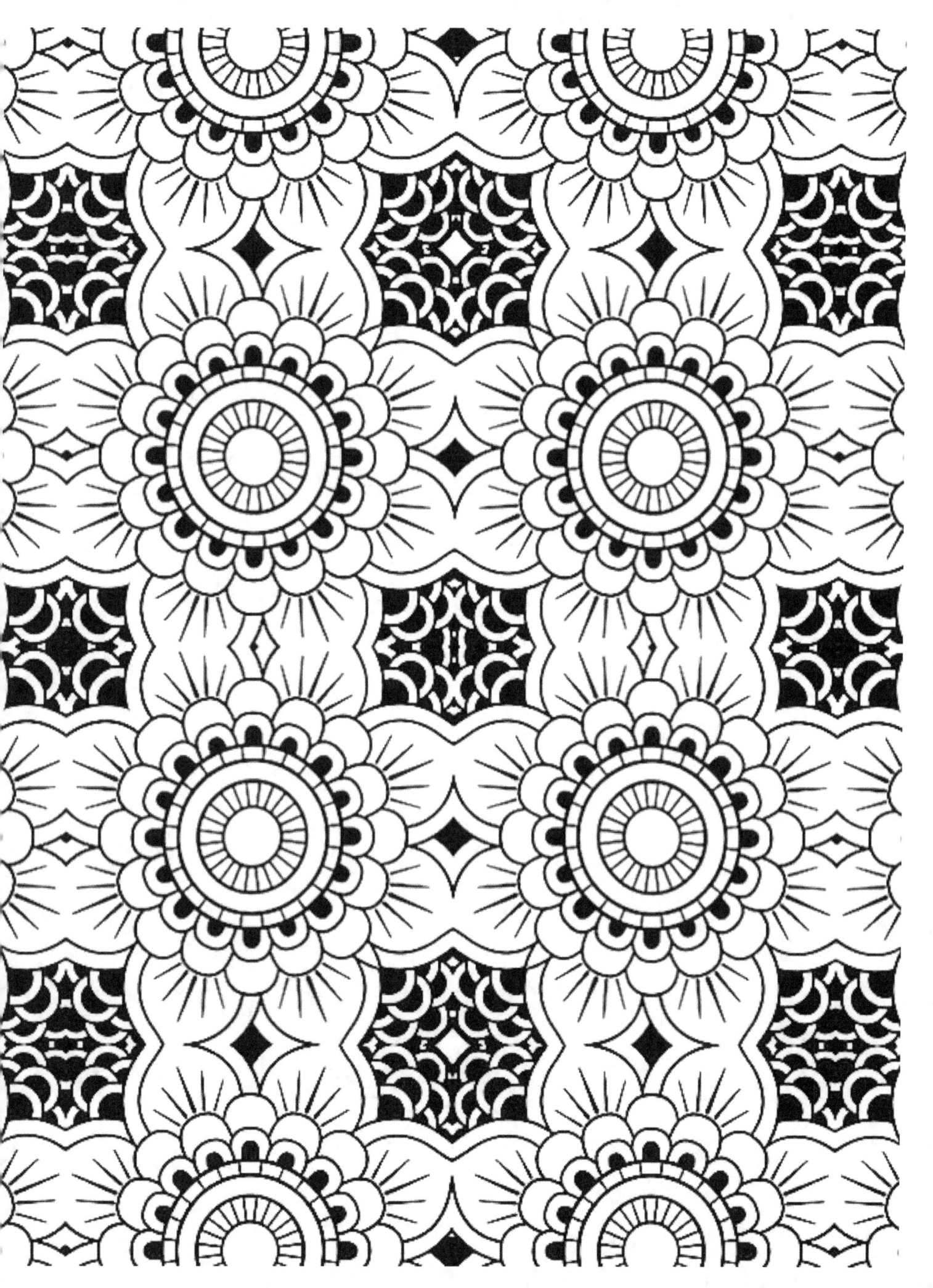

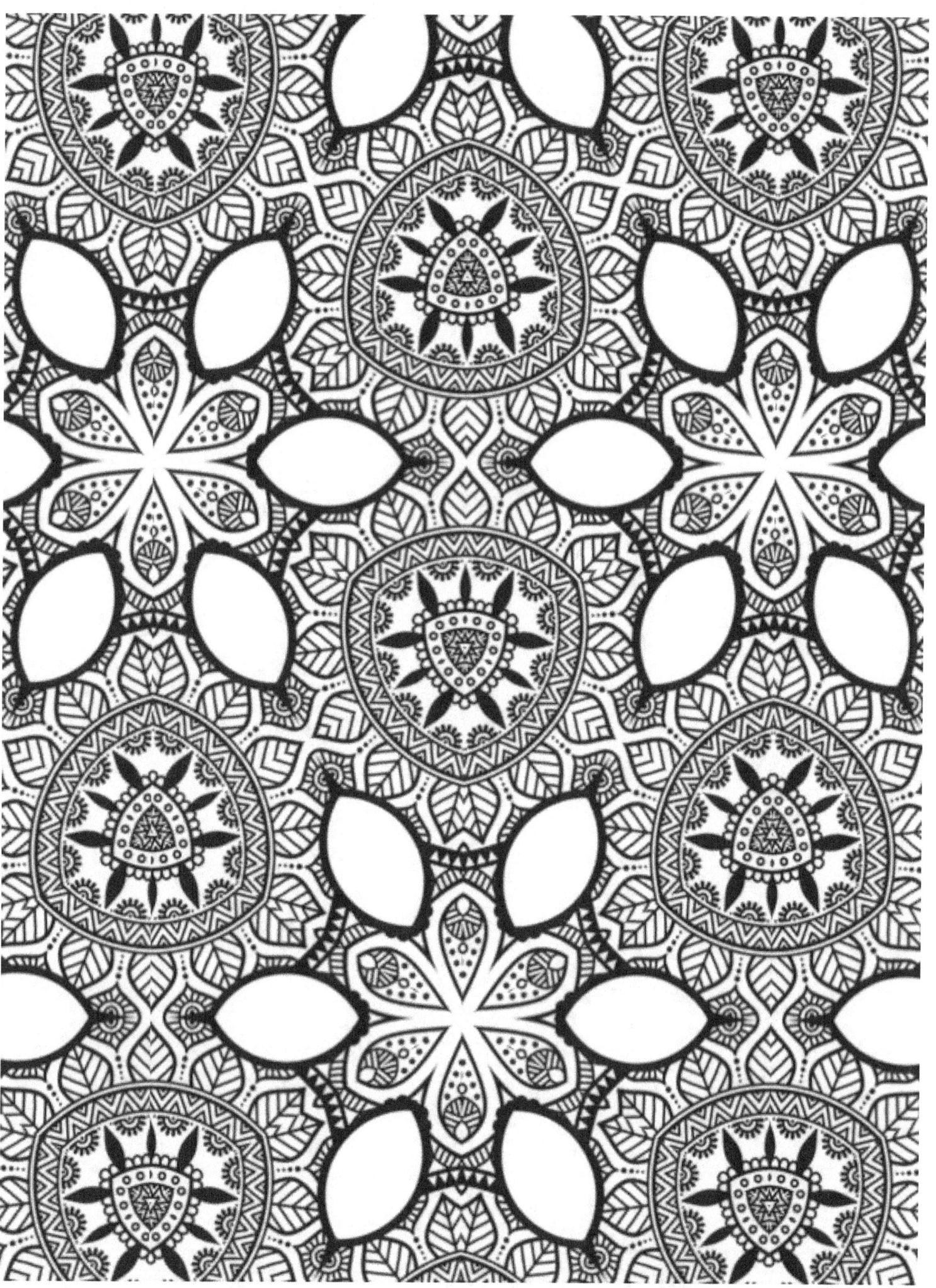

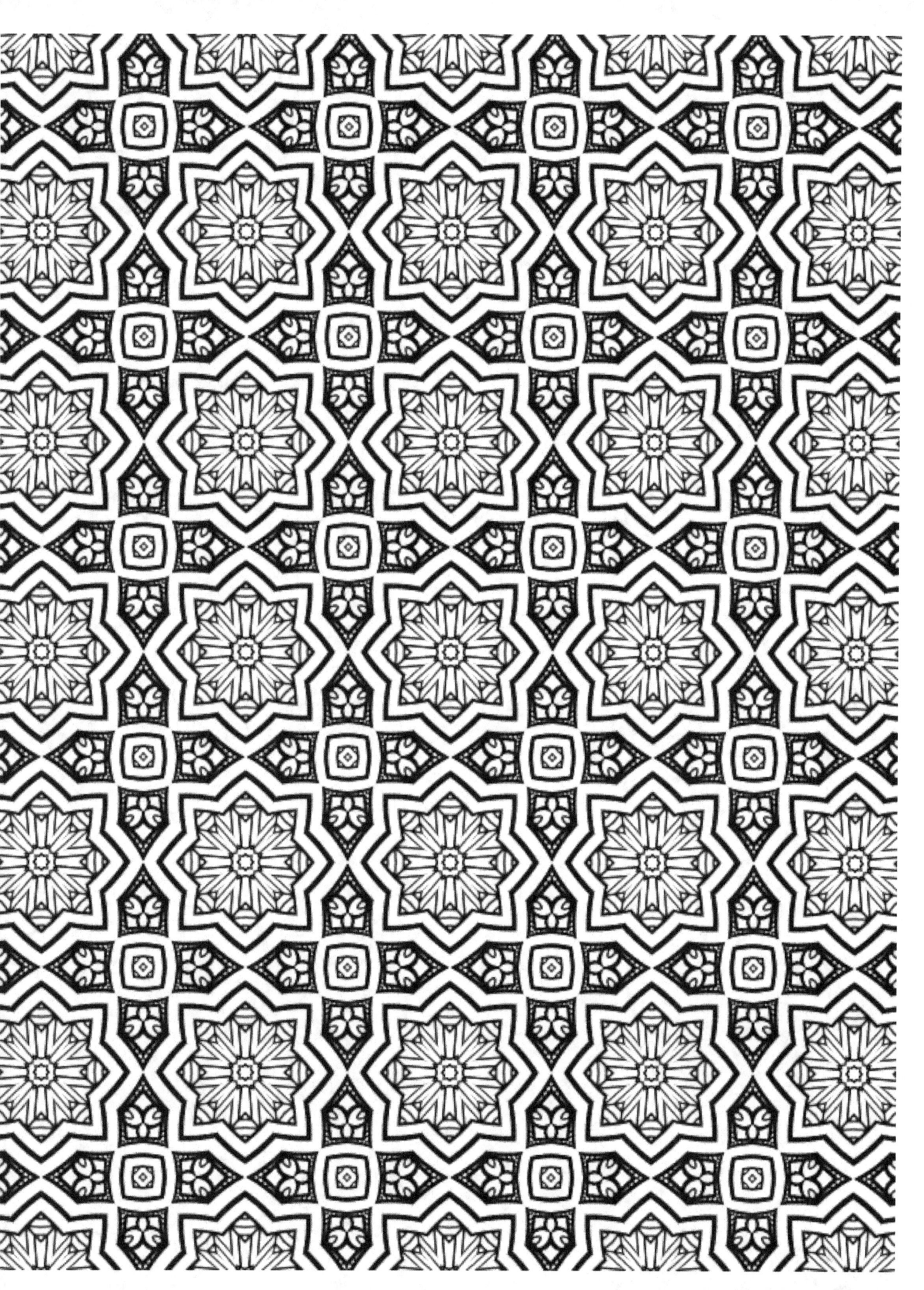